Chapter 1: Understanding Self-Worth

Defining Self-Worth

Defining self-worth is an essential step on the journey toward self-discovery and personal empowerment. Self-worth is not merely a reflection of external accomplishments or social status; it stems from an intrinsic understanding of one's value as a person. It involves recognizing that each individual possesses unique qualities and strengths that contribute to their overall being. This awareness allows individuals to cultivate a sense of worth that is independent of validation from others, leading to healthier relationships and a more fulfilling life.

Awakening Your Inner Worth: A Journey to Self-Discovery

To truly define self-worth, one must engage in self-reflection and examine the beliefs and narratives that have shaped their self-perception. Often, societal standards and external pressures can distort an individual's view of themselves. Techniques such as journaling provide a powerful avenue for self-exploration, enabling individuals to identify negative thought patterns and replace them with affirming and positive self-talk. By documenting thoughts and feelings, one can uncover the root causes of low self-esteem and begin to dismantle the barriers that hinder self-acceptance.

Mindfulness plays a vital role in the process of defining self-worth. Practicing mindfulness encourages individuals to remain present and develop an awareness of their thoughts, feelings, and bodily sensations without judgment. This practice fosters a deeper connection with oneself, allowing for a clearer understanding of personal values and desires. By embracing mindfulness, individuals can cultivate self-compassion, which is essential in recognizing their inherent worth, even in moments of struggle or self-doubt.

Awakening Your Inner Worth: A Journey to Self-Discovery

Overcoming imposter syndrome is another critical aspect of defining self-worth. Many individuals experience feelings of inadequacy and self-doubt despite evident accomplishments. It is crucial to challenge these feelings by acknowledging achievements and recognizing the skills that have contributed to personal and professional successes. Embracing one's journey, including setbacks and triumphs, reinforces the notion that self-worth is not contingent upon perfection but rather on the continuous pursuit of growth and authenticity.

Ultimately, defining self-worth is a dynamic and ongoing process that requires commitment and self-reflection. Engaging in personal development workshops, seeking coaching for career confidence, and practicing creative expression can enhance one's understanding of self-worth. By integrating these strategies into daily life, individuals can foster a deeper connection with themselves, leading to empowerment and a more profound appreciation of their unique contributions to the world. Embracing one's worth is not just a personal victory; it is a transformative experience that enriches relationships and paves the way for a more fulfilling life.

The Importance of Recognizing Your Value

Recognizing your value is a crucial step in the journey toward self-discovery and personal empowerment. Many adults grapple with feelings of inadequacy and self-doubt, often influenced by societal standards and external expectations. When individuals fail to acknowledge their inherent worth, they risk falling into the traps of imposter syndrome and low self-esteem. Understanding your value is not merely an intellectual exercise; it is a transformative process that lays the groundwork for building healthy relationships, pursuing fulfilling careers, and achieving personal growth. By embracing your unique strengths and contributions, you can cultivate a life that reflects your true self.

Awakening Your Inner Worth: A Journey to Self-Discovery

Self-discovery techniques play a vital role in uncovering and recognizing your value. Engaging in practices such as mindfulness and journaling allows for introspection and reflection, enabling you to identify your passions, strengths, and the qualities that set you apart. Mindfulness encourages you to be present with your thoughts and feelings, reducing the noise of self-criticism and external judgments. Journaling serves as a powerful tool for self-reflection, helping you articulate your achievements and experiences that demonstrate your worth. These practices not only foster self-acceptance but also empower you to embrace your individuality and the unique perspective you bring to the world.

Building healthy relationships is intricately tied to recognizing your value. When you understand and appreciate your worth, you naturally attract connections that reflect this understanding. Healthy relationships are founded on mutual respect and appreciation, and when you acknowledge your value, you set the standard for how others should treat you. Conversely, not recognizing your worth may lead to unhealthy dynamics, where you may tolerate disrespect or settle for less than you deserve. By valuing yourself, you create boundaries that safeguard your well-being and encourage others to do the same, fostering relationships that uplift and support your journey.

Overcoming imposter syndrome is another significant aspect of recognizing your value. Many individuals, despite their accomplishments, may feel like frauds or believe they do not deserve their successes. This mindset can be debilitating and hinder personal and professional growth. Acknowledging your value is essential in combating these feelings; it helps you internalize your achievements and recognize that you are deserving of every accolade. Engaging in positive self-talk and utilizing affirmations can reinforce this recognition, allowing you to shift your narrative from self-doubt to self-empowerment. By embracing your accomplishments and understanding that they are a testament to your abilities, you can dismantle the barriers imposed by imposter syndrome.

Ultimately, recognizing your value is an empowering journey that opens the door to personal development and creative expression. As you learn to appreciate your worth, you will find greater confidence in navigating life transitions and pursuing new opportunities. This newfound sense of self will not only enhance your personal and professional relationships but will also inspire you to express yourself creatively. Embracing your value allows you to share your unique voice and perspective with the world, fostering a sense of fulfillment and purpose. By committing to this journey of self-discovery, you empower yourself to live authentically and unapologetically, transforming your life and the lives of those around you.

Common Misconceptions About Self-Worth

Awakening Your Inner Worth: A Journey to Self-Discovery

The concept of self-worth is often clouded by misconceptions that can hinder personal growth and self-acceptance. One prevalent misconception is the belief that self-worth is contingent upon external validation. Many individuals equate their value with achievements, social status, or the approval of others. This perspective diminishes the intrinsic nature of self-worth, which should stem from within, independent of external circumstances. Understanding that self-worth is inherent and not defined by external metrics is essential for cultivating a stable sense of value.

Another common misunderstanding is that self-worth is synonymous with arrogance or narcissism. Some individuals fear that acknowledging their worth may lead to an inflated sense of self or entitlement. However, true self-worth is grounded in humility and self-awareness. It allows individuals to recognize their strengths and weaknesses without the need to compare themselves to others. Embracing one's worth fosters a healthy self-esteem that is balanced and resilient, empowering individuals to engage with the world authentically and compassionately.

Furthermore, many people mistakenly believe that self-worth is a fixed trait that cannot be changed. This notion can lead to a defeatist attitude, where individuals feel trapped in their perceived limitations. In reality, self-worth can evolve through personal development and self-discovery practices. Engaging in activities such as journaling, mindfulness, and coaching can help individuals reassess their beliefs about themselves, leading to a more accurate and empowering understanding of their worth. This dynamic nature of self-worth underscores the importance of continuous self-exploration and growth.

The misconception that self-worth is only relevant in the context of personal success can also be detrimental. Many individuals tend to overlook the significance of self-worth during challenging times or life transitions. Recognizing one's worth, especially in moments of struggle, is crucial for resilience and recovery. By affirming their value regardless of circumstances, individuals can navigate adversity with greater confidence and clarity. This approach not only aids in personal healing but also enhances relationships, as individuals who understand their worth are better equipped to build healthy connections with others.

Finally, the belief that self-worth is a solitary journey is another misconception that can limit personal growth. While self-discovery is indeed an individual process, it is often enriched by supportive relationships and community engagement. Sharing experiences and insights with others can provide valuable perspectives that facilitate a deeper understanding of self-worth. By participating in personal development workshops, group coaching, or creative expression, individuals can cultivate a sense of belonging and collective empowerment, reinforcing their journey toward recognizing and embracing their inherent value.

Chapter 2: Techniques for Self-Discovery

Exploring Your Core Values

Awakening Your Inner Worth: A Journey to Self-Discovery

Exploring your core values is a vital step in the journey of self-discovery and personal development. Core values serve as the guiding principles that shape your decisions, behaviors, and relationships. Understanding these values helps you recognize what truly matters to you, allowing for greater clarity and purpose in your life. By identifying your core values, you can create a framework that supports your aspirations and reinforces your sense of self-worth, ultimately leading to more fulfilling experiences both personally and professionally.

To begin this exploration, consider engaging in reflective practices such as journaling or meditation. Set aside dedicated time to contemplate what you believe is most important in your life. You might ask yourself questions like, "What qualities do I admire in others?" or "What experiences have made me feel most fulfilled?" Writing down your thoughts can help clarify your feelings and illuminate patterns that reveal your intrinsic values. This process not only enhances self-awareness but also fosters mindfulness, allowing you to better understand how your values influence your daily choices and interactions.

Awakening Your Inner Worth: A Journey to Self-Discovery

As you identify your core values, it can be helpful to categorize them into different areas of your life, such as personal, professional, and relational values. Personal values may include integrity, compassion, or creativity, while professional values could encompass ambition, innovation, or collaboration. Relational values, on the other hand, might involve trust, respect, and loyalty. By breaking down your values into these categories, you can see how they align with your current life circumstances and where adjustments may be necessary to live more authentically.

Once you have a clearer understanding of your core values, reflect on how they manifest in your relationships and interactions with others. Are you surrounded by people who share similar values, or do you often find yourself in situations that conflict with what you hold dear? Building healthy relationships is easier when you are aware of your values and can communicate them effectively. This awareness not only helps you set boundaries but also empowers you to seek connections that resonate with your true self, enhancing both your personal and professional life.

Finally, remember that the journey of exploring your core values is ongoing. As you navigate life transitions and face new challenges, your values may evolve. Regularly revisiting and reassessing your values through practices such as coaching or affirmations can support your growth and reinforce your confidence. Embrace the process of self-discovery as a means of empowerment, allowing your core values to guide you toward a more authentic and fulfilling existence.

Identifying Passions and Interests

Identifying passions and interests is a crucial step in the journey of self-discovery, particularly for adults seeking to understand their worth and value in both personal and professional realms. This process involves introspection and exploration, allowing individuals to connect with what truly resonates within them. By recognizing and embracing their passions, adults can cultivate a sense of purpose that fosters personal growth and enhances their relationships. Engaging with these interests not only enriches one's life but also acts as a catalyst for building self-confidence and overcoming feelings of inadequacy.

To begin identifying passions, it is beneficial to explore past experiences and activities that have brought joy and fulfillment. Reflecting on moments in life when one felt energized or excited can provide valuable insights into what truly matters. Journaling serves as an effective technique in this regard, enabling individuals to articulate their thoughts and feelings. By writing about experiences that evoked strong emotions, one can create a clearer picture of interests that align with their core values. This reflection not only aids in recognizing passions but also assists in developing a narrative of self-worth that is empowering and authentic.

Mindfulness practices can further enhance the exploration of passions and interests. By cultivating present-moment awareness, individuals can observe their thoughts, feelings, and reactions to various activities without judgment. This heightened awareness can reveal hidden interests and passions that may have been overlooked in the hustle of daily life. Engaging in mindfulness encourages self-acceptance, allowing individuals to embrace their unique preferences and curiosities without the fear of societal expectations or external validation. This non-judgmental exploration fosters a deeper connection to one's inner self, paving the way for a more fulfilling life.

As individuals begin to identify their passions, it is essential to consider how these interests can be integrated into daily life. Building healthy relationships often involves sharing passions with others, creating opportunities for connection and collaboration. Whether through joining clubs, attending workshops, or participating in community events, engaging with like-minded individuals can enhance the experience of pursuing interests. This sense of community not only supports personal growth but also reinforces a positive self-image, combating feelings of isolation or imposter syndrome that may arise when pursuing new endeavors.

Lastly, empowerment through creative expression plays a vital role in solidifying one's passions and interests. Whether through art, writing, music, or any form of creativity, expressing oneself can lead to profound self-discovery and acceptance. These creative outlets provide a safe space for individuals to explore their feelings and thoughts, often leading to unexpected revelations about what they value most. Embracing creativity as a means of self-exploration not only fosters a deeper understanding of personal interests but also nurtures a sense of self-worth that enhances every aspect of life, from career choices to relationships.

The Role of Introspection

Awakening Your Inner Worth: A Journey to Self-Discovery

Introspection serves as a vital tool in the journey of self-discovery, allowing individuals to delve deep into their thoughts, emotions, and experiences. By engaging in introspective practices, adults can gain a clearer understanding of their values, beliefs, and motivations. This self-examination fosters a deeper connection to one's inner self, enabling individuals to identify their worth and value in both personal and professional spheres. As individuals reflect on their life experiences, they are better equipped to navigate the complexities of relationships, career transitions, and personal growth.

Through the lens of mindfulness, introspection encourages individuals to observe their thoughts without judgment. This non-reactive awareness creates a safe space for self-reflection, allowing people to confront their fears, aspirations, and the often debilitating feelings associated with imposter syndrome. By acknowledging these feelings, individuals can dismantle the barriers that prevent them from recognizing their inherent worth. This process not only promotes self-acceptance but also lays the groundwork for building healthy relationships with oneself and others.

Awakening Your Inner Worth: A Journey to Self-Discovery

Journaling is one of the most effective introspective techniques, providing a structured way to articulate thoughts and emotions. Writing allows individuals to externalize their inner dialogues, making it easier to identify patterns and areas for growth. Through regular journaling, individuals can track their progress, celebrate successes, and articulate their challenges. This practice not only reinforces positive self-talk but also enhances clarity in decision-making, empowering individuals to pursue their passions and goals with confidence.

Coaching for career confidence often incorporates introspective methodologies, guiding individuals to uncover their strengths and aspirations. By exploring their professional journey through introspection, clients can align their career paths with their core values. This alignment fosters a sense of purpose and fulfillment, essential components of self-worth. As individuals become more attuned to their professional identity, they can navigate career transitions with greater ease and assurance, ensuring that their choices reflect their true selves.

Ultimately, the role of introspection in personal development cannot be overstated. It acts as a catalyst for empowerment through creative expression, allowing individuals to explore their identities and potential. By embracing introspective practices, adults can cultivate a profound sense of self-worth that enhances all areas of life, from personal relationships to professional endeavors. This journey of self-discovery is not merely about understanding oneself; it is about celebrating one's unique contributions to the world and embracing the fullness of one's being.

Chapter 3: Building Healthy Relationships

Understanding Relationship Dynamics

Awakening Your Inner Worth: A Journey to Self-Discovery

Understanding relationship dynamics is essential for anyone seeking to enhance their self-worth and build healthier connections with others. Relationships serve as mirrors, reflecting back our perceptions of ourselves and the world around us. By examining the intricacies of these dynamics, individuals can gain insight into their own behaviors, beliefs, and emotional responses. Recognizing patterns within our interactions enables us to break free from unhealthy cycles and fosters an environment where self-discovery can flourish.

At the core of relationship dynamics lies the concept of reciprocity. Healthy relationships thrive on mutual respect, understanding, and support. When both parties are committed to nurturing the relationship, it transforms into a space for growth and empowerment. Conversely, imbalanced dynamics, where one person consistently takes while the other gives, can lead to resentment and disconnection. By identifying these patterns, adults can take proactive steps to establish boundaries, communicate needs, and foster relationships that honor mutual worth.

Another crucial aspect of relationship dynamics is the role of self-acceptance. Individuals who struggle with imposter syndrome may find it particularly challenging to engage authentically with others. They may project insecurities or fear of inadequacy, which can hinder emotional intimacy and trust. By cultivating mindfulness practices and engaging in positive self-talk, individuals can shift their internal narratives. This newfound confidence allows for more genuine interactions, creating a foundation for deeper connections and healthier relationships.

Furthermore, the process of self-reflection through journaling can unveil the subconscious beliefs that shape our relationship dynamics. Writing about experiences, feelings, and patterns not only enhances self-awareness but also reveals underlying motivations and fears. This practice can lead to transformative insights, allowing individuals to confront and dismantle limiting beliefs. By understanding the roots of their actions and reactions, adults can engage in personal development workshops or coaching sessions to further explore and refine their relationship dynamics.

Ultimately, empowering oneself through creative expression can also significantly influence relationship dynamics. Engaging in artistic endeavors allows for the exploration of emotions and experiences that may be difficult to articulate verbally. This form of self-expression can bridge gaps in communication, enhancing understanding between individuals. As adults embark on their journeys of self-discovery, recognizing and reshaping their relationship dynamics becomes a pivotal step towards embracing their inner worth and fostering meaningful connections with others.

Setting Boundaries

Setting boundaries is a crucial aspect of recognizing and affirming your self-worth. Boundaries define the limits of what you will accept from others and what you expect in return. They are essential for maintaining healthy relationships, fostering personal growth, and ensuring emotional well-being. By establishing clear boundaries, you protect your time, energy, and mental health, allowing you to engage in self-discovery and affirm your value in every interaction.

To set effective boundaries, it is important to engage in self-reflection. Consider what areas of your life feel unbalanced or overwhelming. Are there relationships that drain your energy or situations that make you uncomfortable? Journaling can be a powerful tool during this process. Write down your thoughts and feelings about these relationships or situations, identifying specific behaviors that you wish to change. This reflective practice not only clarifies your needs but also reinforces your commitment to your own worth.

Communicating boundaries can often be challenging, especially if you are not accustomed to asserting your needs. However, it is essential to express your boundaries clearly and respectfully. Use "I" statements to convey how certain behaviors affect you, such as "I feel overwhelmed when I take on additional tasks at work." This approach minimizes defensiveness from others and opens the door for constructive dialogue. Remember, setting boundaries is not about shutting others out but rather about inviting healthier interactions into your life.

Once you have established your boundaries, consistency is key. It can be tempting to compromise your limits in the face of pressure or guilt, but doing so undermines your self-worth. Reinforce your boundaries by practicing mindfulness; stay attuned to your feelings and instincts. If you notice discomfort when your boundaries are tested, take a moment to reassess and reiterate your needs. This practice not only strengthens your resolve but also communicates to others that your boundaries are non-negotiable.

Lastly, embrace the empowerment that comes from setting boundaries. Recognize that asserting your needs is a vital form of self-care, essential for personal development and building healthy relationships. Each time you uphold your boundaries, you reaffirm your value and cultivate a sense of confidence that can help you overcome imposter syndrome. By prioritizing your well-being, you create space for authentic connections and meaningful growth, enabling you to navigate life transitions with grace and assurance.

Communicating Effectively

Effective communication is a cornerstone of personal development, particularly when it comes to understanding and expressing one's self-worth. It begins with self-awareness, which enables individuals to articulate their thoughts and feelings accurately. When you are attuned to your own needs and values, you can convey them with clarity and confidence. This self-awareness fosters authentic connections with others, allowing you to engage in meaningful dialogues that reflect your true self. Practicing active listening enhances this process, as it encourages openness and understanding in conversations, making it easier to navigate relationships while affirming your worth.

Building healthy relationships is significantly influenced by how we communicate. When we express ourselves honestly and respectfully, we invite others to do the same. This mutual exchange creates a safe space for vulnerability, which is essential for deepening connections. Moreover, effective communication helps mitigate misunderstandings and conflicts, which can often arise from a lack of clarity. By employing techniques such as "I" statements and reflective listening, individuals can express their feelings without placing blame, fostering an environment where both parties feel valued and heard. This approach not only strengthens relationships but also reinforces one's self-worth through positive interactions.

Overcoming imposter syndrome is another area where effective communication plays a vital role. Many individuals struggle with feelings of inadequacy, often fearing exposure as a fraud despite their accomplishments. Openly discussing these feelings with trusted peers or mentors can diminish their power. Sharing experiences and seeking validation from others can remind individuals of their value and capabilities. In addition, incorporating positive self-talk and affirmations into daily communication can shift internal narratives, reinforcing a sense of belonging and competence. This shift is crucial for building self-esteem and pursuing personal and professional goals with confidence.

Mindfulness enhances effective communication by encouraging individuals to remain present during interactions. Practicing mindfulness allows for a deeper understanding of one's emotions and reactions, which can significantly impact how one communicates. When individuals approach conversations with a mindful attitude, they are more likely to respond thoughtfully rather than react impulsively. This not only improves the quality of communication but also promotes self-acceptance, as individuals learn to express their thoughts and feelings without judgment. Mindfulness can be integrated into personal development workshops and journaling exercises, providing practical tools for enhancing communication skills.

Finally, empowerment through creative expression can serve as a powerful vehicle for effective communication. Engaging in artistic endeavors allows individuals to explore and articulate their inner thoughts and feelings in unique ways. Whether through writing, visual arts, or performing, creative expression can unlock new pathways for communication that transcend traditional verbal interactions. This form of expression fosters self-discovery, enabling individuals to connect with their inner worth and share it with the world. Through workshops and coaching, individuals can harness their creative abilities to enhance their communication skills, ultimately leading to a more fulfilling and authentic self-expression.

Chapter 4: Overcoming Imposter Syndrome

Recognizing Imposter Feelings

Awakening Your Inner Worth: A Journey to Self-Discovery

Recognizing imposter feelings is a crucial step in the journey toward self-discovery and self-acceptance. Many adults experience moments of doubt and insecurity, often questioning their abilities and worth despite evidence of their achievements. These feelings can manifest as a persistent fear of being exposed as a fraud, leading to anxiety and a reluctance to fully engage in personal and professional opportunities. Recognizing these emotions is the first step to overcoming them and embracing one's true self-worth.

Imposter syndrome can often be triggered by high expectations, both self-imposed and external. Adults may find themselves in competitive environments, whether at work or in social circles, where their achievements feel inadequate compared to those around them. This phenomenon is not limited to any specific demographic; it transcends age, gender, and professional background. Acknowledging that these feelings are common can help alleviate the isolation that individuals may feel, reinforcing the idea that they are not alone in their experiences.

Mindfulness practices can serve as powerful tools in recognizing and addressing imposter feelings. By cultivating awareness of one's thoughts and emotions, individuals can begin to identify the patterns that contribute to feelings of inadequacy. Journaling can be particularly effective, allowing for self-reflection and the exploration of underlying beliefs that fuel these emotions. Writing about achievements, strengths, and moments of confidence can provide a clearer perspective on one's capabilities, helping to counteract the negative self-talk often associated with imposter feelings.

Building healthy relationships is another vital aspect of recognizing and overcoming imposter syndrome. Surrounding oneself with supportive individuals who celebrate successes, no matter how small, fosters an environment of encouragement and validation. Engaging in open conversations about feelings of self-doubt can demystify these emotions, allowing others to share their own experiences and strategies for overcoming similar challenges. This collective support bolsters personal growth and reinforces the notion that everyone grapples with self-doubt at times.

Ultimately, recognizing imposter feelings is about embracing vulnerability and taking actionable steps toward personal development. Affirmations and positive self-talk can significantly shift one's mindset, providing a counter-narrative to the inner critic that often accompanies imposter syndrome. Empowerment through creative expression, whether through art, writing, or other forms, allows individuals to articulate their experiences and feelings, transforming doubt into a source of strength. As adults navigate life transitions and seek to enhance their self-worth, recognizing and addressing imposter feelings becomes an essential component of their journey toward self-discovery and fulfillment.

Strategies to Combat Self-Doubt

Self-doubt is a pervasive challenge that can hinder personal growth and impede the realization of one's potential. To effectively combat self-doubt, individuals must first engage in self-reflection, allowing them to identify the root causes of their insecurities. This process often involves journaling, a powerful tool for self-discovery. By documenting thoughts and feelings, individuals can gain clarity on their self-perceptions and the narratives they create about their worth. This practice not only illuminates the specific triggers of self-doubt but also establishes a foundation for understanding and accepting one's identity.

Another vital strategy is the implementation of positive self-talk and affirmations. Individuals can rewire their thought patterns by consciously replacing negative self-statements with positive affirmations. This practice reinforces the belief in one's capabilities and inherent worth. Regularly affirming strengths and achievements can create a more balanced self-image, helping to diminish feelings of inadequacy. Engaging in this exercise daily cultivates a mindset of empowerment, gradually shifting the internal dialogue from self-criticism to self-acceptance and encouragement.

Building healthy relationships is another essential element in combating self-doubt. Surrounding oneself with supportive individuals who recognize and appreciate one's value fosters an environment conducive to growth. These relationships provide not only affirmation but also constructive feedback, which can help individuals see themselves more clearly. In contrast, distancing from toxic relationships that perpetuate feelings of inadequacy is crucial. By fostering connections that uplift and inspire, individuals can reinforce their sense of worth and diminish the impact of self-doubt.

Mindfulness and self-acceptance serve as foundational practices in navigating self-doubt. Mindfulness encourages individuals to stay present and observe their thoughts without judgment. This awareness allows for a pause between the emergence of self-doubt and the reaction to it, creating space for a more rational and compassionate response. Embracing self-acceptance, on the other hand, involves acknowledging imperfections and recognizing that everyone experiences self-doubt at times. This understanding can alleviate the pressure to be flawless and facilitate a more compassionate view of oneself.

Lastly, engaging in creative expression can be a powerful outlet for combating self-doubt. Whether through art, writing, music, or any other form of creativity, self-expression allows individuals to explore and communicate their feelings. This exploration can lead to profound insights about oneself and serve as a reminder of one's unique talents and contributions. Creative expression not only fosters a sense of accomplishment but also can inspire resilience, reinforcing the belief that one's worth is not diminished by moments of uncertainty. By integrating these strategies into daily life, individuals can cultivate a strong sense of self-worth and navigate the complexities of self-doubt with confidence.

Celebrating Achievements

Celebrating achievements is an essential aspect of recognizing one's self-worth and fostering a deeper understanding of personal value. In the journey of self-discovery, acknowledging milestones—big or small—serves as a powerful affirmation of growth and progress. Each achievement reflects the efforts invested in personal development and the courage to confront challenges. By consciously celebrating these moments, individuals reinforce their sense of identity and validate their experiences, which is crucial in overcoming feelings of inadequacy that often accompany imposter syndrome.

The practice of celebrating achievements can take many forms, from private reflections to public acknowledgments. Engaging in mindfulness techniques, such as journaling, allows individuals to document their successes and the emotions associated with them. Writing about achievements not only helps in reinforcing positive self-talk but also serves as a tangible reminder of the journey taken. This reflective practice can illuminate patterns of resilience and strength, encouraging individuals to continue pursuing their goals with confidence and clarity.

In interpersonal relationships, celebrating the achievements of others fosters a supportive environment that enhances collective growth. Recognizing the accomplishments of friends, family, or colleagues strengthens bonds and promotes a culture of encouragement. This practice nurtures healthy relationships by shifting the focus from competition to collaboration, wherein each person's success is viewed as a shared victory. Such an environment cultivates mutual respect and admiration, which are vital components in building self-esteem and confidence.

Creative expression also plays a significant role in celebrating achievements. Engaging in artistic endeavors, whether through painting, writing, or music, allows individuals to channel their experiences into a form that resonates deeply with their emotions. This empowerment through creative expression not only honors personal milestones but also invites others to share in the journey. As individuals share their stories through art, they inspire those around them to recognize and celebrate their own achievements, creating a ripple effect of positivity and self-acceptance.

Ultimately, the celebration of achievements is not merely about recognizing success; it is about embracing the journey of self-discovery and growth. Each acknowledgment serves as a building block in constructing a robust sense of self-worth that transcends external validation. By consistently celebrating accomplishments, individuals reinforce their intrinsic value, cultivate resilience, and inspire a mindset of abundance. This practice empowers them to navigate life transitions with grace and confidence, fostering a profound understanding of their worth in every aspect of life.

Chapter 5: Mindfulness and Self-Acceptance

The Practice of Mindfulness

Awakening Your Inner Worth: A Journey to Self-Discovery

The practice of mindfulness serves as a profound tool in the journey of self-discovery and personal growth. By cultivating present-moment awareness, individuals can transcend the noise of daily life, allowing for a deeper connection with their thoughts, emotions, and intrinsic worth. Mindfulness encourages a non-judgmental observation of the self, fostering an environment where personal insights can flourish. This approach not only enhances self-awareness but also paves the way for accepting oneself fully, which is essential in overcoming feelings of unworthiness often tied to imposter syndrome.

Engaging in mindfulness practices can take various forms, including meditation, mindful breathing, and even mindful movement such as yoga. These techniques help individuals anchor themselves in the present, reducing anxiety and self-doubt that may arise from past experiences or future uncertainties. By dedicating time to these practices, individuals can create a safe space for reflection, allowing for a clearer understanding of their values, strengths, and areas for growth. This clarity can significantly aid in building healthy relationships, as individuals become more attuned to their own needs and the needs of others.

Journaling is another powerful method of integrating mindfulness into daily routines. Writing allows for a structured reflection on thoughts and feelings, providing an opportunity to process experiences and emotions. By combining mindfulness with journaling, individuals can explore their inner landscapes without the constraints of external judgments. This practice not only enhances self-acceptance but also encourages the use of affirmations and positive self-talk, reinforcing a positive self-image and promoting confidence in one's abilities.

As individuals navigate life transitions, mindfulness becomes an invaluable ally. It equips them with the tools needed to face change with grace and resilience. By remaining present and engaged in the moment, individuals can better manage the uncertainties that accompany transitions, whether they are personal or professional. This adaptability fosters empowerment, allowing individuals to embrace new opportunities with a renewed sense of confidence and purpose.

In conclusion, the practice of mindfulness is integral to awakening one's inner worth and embarking on a journey of self-discovery. By fostering present-moment awareness, engaging in reflective practices, and embracing change with an open heart, individuals can cultivate a deeper connection to their true selves. This journey not only enhances personal development but also empowers individuals to build meaningful relationships and navigate life's challenges with confidence and grace.

Cultivating Self-Compassion

Cultivating self-compassion is an essential practice for adults seeking to enhance their self-worth and navigate the complexities of personal development. In a world that often prioritizes achievement and perfection, it is crucial to recognize that self-kindness is a powerful antidote to the harsh inner critic that many experience. Self-compassion involves treating oneself with the same care and understanding that one would offer to a friend in times of difficulty. This practice not only fosters a more positive relationship with oneself but also lays the groundwork for authentic self-discovery and acceptance.

Awakening Your Inner Worth: A Journey to Self-Discovery

To cultivate self-compassion, it is vital to first acknowledge the common humanity that connects us all. Many adults grapple with feelings of inadequacy and self-doubt, often exacerbated by societal pressures and expectations. Understanding that these feelings are shared can alleviate the isolation that often accompanies them. By recognizing that imperfection is a part of the human experience, individuals can begin to develop a more compassionate view of themselves, allowing for greater emotional resilience and openness to growth.

Mindfulness plays a pivotal role in fostering self-compassion. By bringing awareness to one's thoughts and feelings without judgment, individuals can learn to observe their inner dialogue and challenge negative self-perceptions. This practice encourages a non-reactive stance toward one's emotional experiences, creating space for self-acceptance rather than self-criticism. Engaging in mindfulness exercises, such as focused breathing or guided meditations, can help adults build the capacity for self-compassion, enabling them to respond to their struggles with kindness rather than harshness.

Journaling serves as another powerful tool for cultivating self-compassion. Through reflective writing, individuals can articulate their thoughts and feelings, providing insight into their personal experiences and challenges. This process allows for a deeper understanding of one's emotional landscape and the factors contributing to self-doubt or imposter syndrome. By documenting moments of self-criticism and reframing them with compassionate responses, adults can actively reshape their internal narratives, reinforcing a sense of worth and validation.

Ultimately, cultivating self-compassion is a transformative journey that empowers individuals to embrace their authentic selves. This practice not only enhances self-worth and personal confidence but also enriches relationships with others. When individuals learn to treat themselves with kindness and understanding, they open the door to healthier interactions, built on mutual respect and empathy. As adults navigate life transitions and pursue personal and professional growth, self-compassion will remain a vital ally, providing the strength and encouragement needed to flourish in an ever-changing world.

Embracing Imperfections

Embracing imperfections is a pivotal step in the journey of self-discovery and personal development. In a world that often glorifies perfection, many individuals find themselves trapped in a cycle of self-doubt and comparison. This mindset can lead to feelings of inadequacy and imposter syndrome, where one feels unworthy of their achievements and constantly questions their abilities. Recognizing that imperfections are a natural part of the human experience allows individuals to shift their perspective and cultivate a deeper sense of self-worth. Accepting imperfections is not a resignation to mediocrity; rather, it is an acknowledgment of the inherent beauty in being human.

Awakening Your Inner Worth: A Journey to Self-Discovery

The practice of mindfulness plays a crucial role in embracing imperfections. By grounding oneself in the present moment, individuals can observe their thoughts and feelings without judgment. This non-judgmental awareness fosters a sense of acceptance, enabling individuals to appreciate their flaws and shortcomings as integral parts of their identity. Mindfulness encourages self-reflection, allowing individuals to confront their insecurities and reframe negative self-talk. By recognizing that everyone has imperfections, it becomes easier to cultivate compassion for oneself and others, ultimately leading to healthier relationships.

Self-acceptance is a fundamental component of personal empowerment. When individuals embrace their imperfections, they liberate themselves from the constraints of societal expectations and the pressure to conform. This liberation fosters authenticity, enabling individuals to express their true selves without fear of judgment. In doing so, they not only enhance their personal relationships but also inspire others to embrace their own imperfections. This ripple effect can create a supportive environment where vulnerability is celebrated, allowing for deeper connections and mutual growth.

Awakening Your Inner Worth: A Journey to Self-Discovery

Journaling serves as an effective tool for exploring and embracing imperfections. Through reflective writing, individuals can document their thoughts and experiences, providing a safe space for self-exploration. This practice encourages individuals to confront their fears and insecurities, ultimately leading to greater self-awareness. As they navigate their journey, individuals can create affirmations and positive self-talk to counteract negative beliefs about their worth. By chronicling their growth and acknowledging their imperfections, they can foster a more positive self-image and reinforce their value.

Embracing imperfections is not only about acceptance but also about empowerment through creative expression. Engaging in creative activities allows individuals to explore their unique perspectives and express their emotions in a tangible way. Whether through art, writing, or other forms of creativity, individuals can channel their imperfections into something meaningful. This process not only fosters self-discovery but also reinforces the idea that imperfections can be sources of strength and inspiration. By celebrating their flaws and vulnerabilities, individuals can transform their narrative, leading to a more enriched understanding of their worth and potential.

Chapter 6: Personal Development Workshops

Finding the Right Workshop

Awakening Your Inner Worth: A Journey to Self-Discovery

Finding the right workshop is a crucial step in your journey to self-discovery and awakening your inner worth. With a plethora of options available, it's essential to identify workshops that align not only with your personal goals but also with your values and learning style. Begin by reflecting on what you hope to achieve. Are you looking to overcome imposter syndrome, build healthier relationships, or enhance your mindfulness practices? A clear understanding of your objectives will guide you in selecting a workshop that resonates with your aspirations.

Researching potential workshops can be an enlightening experience. Explore various platforms and communities that focus on personal development. Online forums, social media groups, and local community centers often provide information on workshops tailored to specific niches such as self-acceptance or creative expression. Pay attention to the credentials and experiences of the facilitators, as their expertise will significantly impact the quality of the workshop. Look for testimonials or reviews from past participants to gauge the effectiveness and relevance of the program.

Consider the structure and format of the workshops you are evaluating. Some individuals thrive in interactive environments, while others may prefer a more introspective setting. Determine whether you are drawn to group sessions that foster community and shared experiences or if one-on-one coaching aligns better with your personal growth style. Additionally, examine the duration and frequency of the workshops. Short-term workshops can provide quick insights, whereas longer programs may offer in-depth exploration and sustained support.

Affordability and accessibility are also key factors in your decision-making process. Workshops can vary widely in cost, and it's important to find options that fit your budget without compromising the quality of the experience. Many organizations offer sliding scale fees or scholarships, making personal development more accessible to a broader audience. Furthermore, consider the location and format of the workshops, whether they are in-person or online. Flexibility in participation can enhance your commitment to the process.

Finally, trust your intuition when selecting a workshop. After conducting thorough research and weighing your options, listen to your inner voice. Does the workshop feel right for you? Are you excited about the opportunity it presents? Engaging in a workshop should inspire growth and empowerment. By finding the right workshop, you are taking an essential step toward embracing your self-worth and embarking on a transformative journey of self-discovery.

Setting Goals for Growth

Setting goals for growth is a fundamental aspect of the journey towards self-discovery and the realization of one's inner worth. In this context, growth is not merely about achieving external milestones but also about fostering a deeper understanding of oneself. By setting intentional and meaningful goals, individuals can create a roadmap that guides them through the complexities of personal development. This process encourages reflection on personal values and aspirations, ultimately leading to a more fulfilled and authentic existence.

Awakening Your Inner Worth: A Journey to Self-Discovery

The first step in setting goals for growth is to engage in self-reflection. This involves examining one's thoughts, feelings, and behaviors to identify areas for improvement and development. Journaling can be an effective tool in this process, allowing individuals to articulate their innermost thoughts and aspirations. Through consistent journaling, patterns can emerge that highlight both strengths and areas that require attention. This self-awareness lays the groundwork for meaningful goal-setting, ensuring that the objectives chosen resonate with one's true self.

Once clarity is achieved through self-reflection, the next step is to formulate specific, measurable, achievable, relevant, and time-bound (SMART) goals. This framework ensures that goals are not only aspirational but also practical and attainable. For instance, someone looking to overcome imposter syndrome might set a goal to engage in positive self-talk daily or participate in a personal development workshop each month. By breaking larger ambitions into smaller, actionable steps, individuals can maintain motivation and track their progress, fostering a sense of accomplishment along the way.

Goal-setting should also incorporate an element of mindfulness, encouraging individuals to remain present in their journey. This means recognizing that growth is not always linear and that setbacks may occur. Embracing mindfulness allows individuals to navigate these challenges with grace and resilience. By practicing self-acceptance, one can appreciate the journey as much as the destination, understanding that each experience contributes to personal growth. This perspective not only enhances the goal-setting process but also cultivates a healthier relationship with oneself.

Lastly, celebrating achievements, no matter how small, is crucial in sustaining motivation and reinforcing self-worth. Acknowledging progress fosters a positive mindset and encourages further exploration of personal potential. Creative expression can also play a vital role in this celebration, allowing individuals to articulate their feelings of accomplishment through art, writing, or other mediums. By intertwining goal-setting with self-reflection, mindfulness, and celebration, individuals can create a robust framework for personal growth that nurtures their inner worth and propels them forward on their journey of self-discovery.

Building a Supportive Community

Building a supportive community is a fundamental aspect of awakening your inner worth and fostering self-discovery. At its core, a supportive community provides a safe environment where individuals can express their thoughts, feelings, and experiences without fear of judgment. This sense of belonging is essential for personal growth, as it enables individuals to explore their identities, values, and aspirations. Engaging with others who share similar journeys can significantly enhance your understanding of self-worth and encourage you to embrace your unique qualities.

To build a supportive community, it is vital to seek out relationships that are based on mutual respect, trust, and understanding. This can be achieved by actively participating in groups or workshops that focus on personal development, self-discovery, and empowerment. Whether through online forums, local meetups, or organized workshops, connecting with like-minded individuals can offer invaluable insights and encouragement. By sharing experiences and challenges, you create a network of support that can help you navigate life's transitions and overcome feelings of inadequacy often associated with imposter syndrome.

Creating a culture of mindfulness and self-acceptance within your community can further enhance its supportive nature. Encouraging practices such as active listening, open communication, and compassion fosters an atmosphere where individuals feel valued and understood. Mindfulness techniques, such as meditation or yoga, can be incorporated into community activities, promoting emotional well-being and reducing stress. As members engage in these practices together, they not only strengthen their bonds but also reinforce the importance of nurturing self-worth and acceptance in each other.

Awakening Your Inner Worth: A Journey to Self-Discovery

Journaling can serve as a powerful tool for self-reflection within a supportive community. By sharing journaling prompts or experiences, members can gain deeper insights into their emotions, motivations, and challenges. This practice not only cultivates personal growth but also encourages vulnerability and openness, essential components for building trust among community members. Facilitating group discussions around journaling can lead to meaningful conversations that reinforce the value of self-exploration and collective support in the journey toward self-discovery.

Empowerment through creative expression is another vital avenue for building a supportive community. Encouraging members to share their artistic talents, whether through writing, visual arts, or performance, can foster a sense of accomplishment and validation. Creative outlets allow individuals to express their inner thoughts and emotions, facilitating deeper connections with others. By celebrating each other's creativity, the community reinforces the idea that each member contributes unique value, further enhancing the overall sense of worth and belonging.

Chapter 7: Journaling for Self-Reflection

Benefits of Journaling

Journaling serves as a powerful tool for self-discovery and personal growth, allowing individuals to explore their thoughts, feelings, and experiences in a structured manner. One of the primary benefits of journaling is the opportunity it provides for self-reflection. By writing regularly, individuals can gain insights into their behaviors, motivations, and emotional responses. This process fosters a deeper understanding of oneself, which is crucial for recognizing and affirming one's worth. As people articulate their thoughts on paper, they often uncover patterns that contribute to their sense of self, ultimately leading to greater self-acceptance and resilience.

Awakening Your Inner Worth: A Journey to Self-Discovery

Another significant advantage of journaling is its role in enhancing emotional intelligence. When individuals engage in the practice of journaling, they become more attuned to their emotions and the underlying reasons for their feelings. This heightened awareness can facilitate healthier relationships, as individuals learn to communicate their thoughts and feelings more effectively. Journaling acts as a safe space for expressing complex emotions, allowing individuals to process feelings of joy, sadness, frustration, and fear without judgment. This emotional clarity can greatly improve interpersonal dynamics, leading to more meaningful connections with others.

Journaling also serves as a practical method for overcoming imposter syndrome, a common challenge faced by many adults. Writing about personal achievements and experiences can help individuals recognize their capabilities and strengths, countering feelings of inadequacy. By documenting successes, no matter how small, individuals can create a tangible record of their accomplishments, reinforcing their sense of worth. This practice not only combats negative self-perceptions but also encourages a mindset shift towards embracing one's unique journey and contributions.

Awakening Your Inner Worth: A Journey to Self-Discovery

In the context of mindfulness and self-acceptance, journaling encourages a present-focused approach to life. When individuals take the time to write about their daily experiences, they cultivate a habit of mindfulness that promotes living in the moment. This practice can reduce stress and anxiety, as it allows individuals to process their thoughts and feelings in real-time. Furthermore, the act of journaling itself can be a form of creative expression, empowering individuals to explore their identities and aspirations without fear of judgment. This creative outlet fosters a sense of empowerment, facilitating personal development and growth.

Finally, journaling can play a crucial role in navigating life transitions. Whether facing changes in career, relationships, or personal circumstances, writing can provide clarity and direction during uncertain times. By articulating their thoughts and feelings about these transitions, individuals can gain insight into their values and priorities, which can inform their decisions moving forward. This reflective practice enables individuals to approach life changes with confidence and intention, reinforcing their inner worth and resilience throughout the journey of self-discovery.

Prompts for Self-Exploration

Prompts for self-exploration are essential tools that facilitate a deeper understanding of oneself. Engaging in self-exploration allows individuals to uncover their beliefs, values, and aspirations, ultimately leading to a clearer sense of self-worth. These prompts serve as a catalyst for introspection, providing the necessary space to reflect on personal experiences and emotions. By dedicating time to respond to these prompts, individuals can gain insights that empower them to navigate life with confidence and clarity.

Awakening Your Inner Worth: A Journey to Self-Discovery

One effective approach to self-exploration is through the practice of journaling. Writing prompts can guide individuals in articulating their thoughts and feelings, creating a tangible expression of their inner landscape. For instance, consider prompts such as "What are three significant experiences that have shaped my self-perception?" or "How do I define my worth beyond external validation?" These questions encourage individuals to delve into their past, identify patterns, and reframe their narratives. As they document their reflections, they foster a greater awareness of their strengths and areas for growth, paving the way for personal development.

Another powerful technique involves mindfulness and self-acceptance. Prompts that encourage individuals to focus on the present moment can enhance their self-awareness and appreciation for their unique qualities. For example, prompts like "What do I appreciate most about myself today?" or "How can I practice self-compassion in moments of self-doubt?" invite individuals to cultivate a positive relationship with themselves. By regularly reflecting on these questions, they can develop a mindset that embraces authenticity and fosters resilience, essential components in overcoming imposter syndrome and building healthy relationships.

Creative expression can also play a crucial role in self-exploration. Art, music, or any form of creativity can serve as a medium to explore one's identity and emotions. Prompts such as "What does my ideal life look like, and how can I express that creatively?" or "How does my creativity reflect my inner worth?" allow individuals to tap into their innate creativity as a means of self-discovery. This exploration not only enhances their self-esteem but also provides a joyful outlet for expressing their values and aspirations.

In navigating life transitions, self-exploration prompts can be instrumental in guiding individuals through uncertainty. Questions like "What do I want to learn from this transition?" or "How can I align my actions with my core values during this change?" empower individuals to take proactive steps toward personal growth. By reflecting on these prompts, they can gain clarity and confidence in their decisions, fostering a sense of empowerment that is vital for adapting to new circumstances. Ultimately, the journey of self-exploration through thoughtful prompts cultivates a deeper understanding of one's worth and the ability to navigate life with purpose and intention.

Creating a Consistent Practice

Awakening Your Inner Worth: A Journey to Self-Discovery

Creating a consistent practice is essential for anyone embarking on a journey of self-discovery and personal growth. Establishing routines that foster self-acceptance, mindfulness, and empowerment can significantly enhance your understanding of self-worth and value. A consistent practice allows you to cultivate habits that reinforce positive self-talk and affirmations, creating a solid foundation for overcoming challenges such as imposter syndrome. By dedicating time each day to these practices, you create a space where self-exploration can thrive, leading to deeper insights and a more profound connection with your inner self.

To begin, identify activities that resonate with you and align with your goals for self-discovery. This may include journaling, meditation, or creative expression. Journaling, in particular, can serve as a powerful tool for self-reflection, helping you articulate your thoughts and emotions. Set aside a specific time each day or week for this practice, allowing yourself the freedom to explore your feelings without judgment. Creating a designated space for reflection can also enhance your experience, making it a sacred ritual that you look forward to as part of your self-care routine.

Awakening Your Inner Worth: A Journey to Self-Discovery

Mindfulness plays a crucial role in establishing a consistent practice. Engage in mindfulness exercises that encourage you to be present in the moment, whether through breathwork, guided meditation, or mindful observation of your surroundings. These practices can help you cultivate awareness of your thoughts and feelings, allowing you to recognize patterns that may contribute to feelings of inadequacy or self-doubt. By integrating mindfulness into your daily routine, you develop a deeper understanding of your emotions, enabling you to respond to challenges with greater clarity and confidence.

Accountability can also enhance the consistency of your practice. Consider joining a personal development workshop or finding a coach who can guide you on your journey. Sharing your experiences with others provides a support system that encourages commitment and growth. Engaging in discussions with like-minded individuals fosters a sense of community, allowing you to learn from one another's insights and experiences. This collaborative approach can further empower you to stay dedicated to your practice, reinforcing your self-worth and building healthy relationships.

Lastly, embrace the idea that consistency does not mean rigidity. Allow your practice to evolve as you grow and change. Be open to experimenting with different techniques and tools, adapting your routine to fit your current needs. This flexibility is vital for maintaining motivation and preventing burnout. Celebrate your progress, no matter how small, and recognize that each step you take on this journey contributes to a greater understanding of your inner worth. By committing to a consistent practice, you empower yourself to navigate life transitions with grace and confidence, ultimately awakening your true potential.

Chapter 8: Coaching for Career Confidence

The Role of a Career Coach

Awakening Your Inner Worth: A Journey to Self-Discovery

The role of a career coach is pivotal in guiding individuals through the complexities of professional development and self-discovery. In an ever-evolving job market, where personal identity and career aspirations often intersect, a career coach serves as a supportive partner in helping clients navigate their paths. They employ various techniques that encourage clients to explore their self-worth and value, fostering an environment where individuals can confront their career-related fears and aspirations. By facilitating discussions on personal strengths, weaknesses, and goals, a career coach empowers clients to articulate their professional identities with clarity and confidence.

Awakening Your Inner Worth: A Journey to Self-Discovery

A career coach utilizes self-discovery techniques to assist clients in identifying their passions and aligning them with their career objectives. This process often involves reflective exercises that help clients uncover their intrinsic motivations and values. By encouraging journaling and self-reflection, a career coach guides individuals to better understand their unique skills and experiences. This introspective journey not only aids in clarifying career goals but also enhances self-acceptance, as clients learn to appreciate their inherent worth beyond external validation. Through this enhanced self-awareness, individuals are better equipped to make informed decisions about their careers.

Awakening Your Inner Worth: A Journey to Self-Discovery

Overcoming imposter syndrome is another critical aspect of a career coach's role. Many clients struggle with feelings of inadequacy and self-doubt, which can hinder their career progression. A skilled coach provides strategies to combat these negative thought patterns through affirmations and positive self-talk. By reframing limiting beliefs and fostering a more empowering narrative, clients can cultivate a mindset that embraces their achievements and potential. This transformation is essential in developing a resilient self-image that supports professional growth and encourages clients to pursue opportunities that resonate with their true selves.

Additionally, a career coach plays a significant role in helping clients build healthy relationships within professional settings. The ability to navigate workplace dynamics and establish supportive connections is crucial for career advancement. Coaches provide tools for effective communication, conflict resolution, and networking, which are vital skills in fostering a positive work environment. By emphasizing the importance of collaboration and mutual respect, a career coach helps clients create and maintain relationships that are not only beneficial for their careers but also contribute to their overall well-being.

Finally, a career coach supports individuals in navigating life transitions, whether they involve changing careers, seeking promotions, or adapting to new roles. These transitions can be challenging, often eliciting feelings of uncertainty and fear. A coach offers guidance and strategies to approach these changes with confidence and resilience. By fostering a mindset of empowerment through creative expression and mindfulness practices, clients can embrace transitions as opportunities for growth rather than obstacles. Ultimately, the role of a career coach is to illuminate the path toward self-discovery and personal development, enabling individuals to awaken their inner worth and confidently pursue their professional aspirations.

Identifying Career Goals

Awakening Your Inner Worth: A Journey to Self-Discovery

Identifying career goals is a fundamental step in the journey of self-discovery, as it allows individuals to align their professional aspirations with their intrinsic values and personal strengths. To embark on this exploration, one must first engage in deep self-reflection. This process involves understanding what truly matters to you, evaluating your passions, skills, and experiences, and recognizing how these elements contribute to your sense of worth. By conducting an honest assessment of your interests and values, you can begin to articulate a vision for your career that resonates with your authentic self.

One effective technique for identifying career goals is journaling. This practice encourages individuals to document their thoughts and feelings about their current career situation, aspirations, and the barriers they perceive. By regularly writing about your experiences, you can uncover recurring themes and patterns that point toward your true desires. Journaling not only serves as a reflective tool but also fosters mindfulness, allowing you to be present with your thoughts and emotions. This awareness is crucial in understanding how your career aligns with your personal identity and self-worth.

Another valuable approach is engaging in personal development workshops or coaching sessions. These structured environments provide opportunities to explore your career aspirations in a supportive community. Coaches and facilitators can guide you through tailored exercises designed to clarify your goals, challenge limiting beliefs, and enhance your confidence. Such interactions promote healthy relationships, as they encourage collaboration and shared experiences with others who are also navigating their career paths. This communal aspect can significantly bolster your motivation and commitment to achieving your goals.

Awakening Your Inner Worth: A Journey to Self-Discovery

Overcoming imposter syndrome is an essential aspect of defining your career objectives. Many individuals struggle with feelings of inadequacy and self-doubt, which can obstruct their ability to pursue meaningful work. Recognizing and addressing these feelings is vital for fostering a positive self-image and embracing your capabilities. Practicing affirmations and positive self-talk can reinforce your self-worth, helping you to visualize your potential and affirm your right to pursue ambitious career goals. This shift in mindset not only empowers you but also enhances your resilience in the face of challenges.

Finally, as you identify your career goals, it is important to remain adaptable and open to change. Life transitions often bring new opportunities and challenges that may require you to reassess your objectives. Embracing this fluidity and allowing yourself the space to pivot can lead to unexpected pathways that align more closely with your evolving self-discovery journey. Empowerment through creative expression can also play a role in this process, as it encourages exploration beyond conventional career paths. By staying attuned to your inner self and being willing to adapt, you can cultivate a fulfilling career that reflects your true worth and aspirations.

Navigating Professional Challenges

Awakening Your Inner Worth: A Journey to Self-Discovery

Navigating professional challenges is an essential aspect of personal development that directly correlates with understanding and affirming your inner worth. In today's dynamic work environment, individuals frequently encounter obstacles that can undermine their confidence and self-esteem. These challenges often manifest as feelings of inadequacy, competition with peers, or the overwhelming pressure to meet expectations. Acknowledging these challenges is the first step toward transforming them into opportunities for growth and self-discovery. By employing self-reflection techniques, individuals can identify their strengths, recognize areas for improvement, and cultivate resilience in the face of adversity.

Self-discovery techniques play a pivotal role in navigating professional challenges. Engaging in practices such as journaling allows individuals to articulate their thoughts and feelings, providing clarity on their experiences. This introspective journey can reveal patterns of behavior and thought processes that may contribute to feelings of inadequacy or imposter syndrome. By documenting their professional experiences, individuals can also track their progress, celebrate their achievements, and develop a more profound sense of self-worth. This practice empowers them to address challenges with a renewed perspective, fostering a mindset that embraces growth rather than fear.

Building healthy relationships within the workplace is another critical component of overcoming professional challenges. Networking and forming connections with colleagues can provide the support system needed to navigate difficult situations. Open communication and collaboration can alleviate feelings of isolation and allow for shared experiences, which can be invaluable in boosting confidence. Engaging in positive self-talk and affirmations can further enhance this process, as these practices reinforce an individual's belief in their capabilities. By cultivating a supportive professional network, individuals can create an environment that encourages mutual growth and fosters resilience.

Mindfulness and self-acceptance are vital tools when facing professional challenges. Practicing mindfulness allows individuals to remain present and focused, reducing anxiety and stress that often accompany workplace pressures. This awareness creates a space for self-acceptance, where individuals can recognize their worth without comparison to others. Embracing imperfections and understanding that everyone faces challenges can alleviate the burden of unrealistic expectations. By integrating mindfulness into their daily routine, individuals can transform their approach to challenges, viewing them as opportunities for learning and development.

Finally, empowerment through creative expression can serve as a powerful means of navigating professional challenges. Engaging in creative activities, whether through art, writing, or other forms of self-expression, can provide an outlet for emotions and a way to process experiences. This creative engagement not only enhances self-awareness but also fosters a sense of achievement and purpose. As individuals explore their creative side, they often discover new strengths and insights that can be applied to professional challenges. Ultimately, by embracing their inner worth and leveraging the tools of self-discovery, individuals can navigate the complexities of their professional lives with confidence and resilience, paving the way for a fulfilling career journey.

Chapter 9: Affirmations and Positive Self-Talk

The Power of Affirmations

Awakening Your Inner Worth: A Journey to Self-Discovery

The concept of affirmations is rooted in the power of positive self-talk, which can significantly influence our mindset and emotional well-being. By consciously choosing words that reflect our values and aspirations, we set the stage for transforming our internal dialogue. This practice is especially vital for adults who are navigating complex life transitions, dealing with imposter syndrome, or seeking to cultivate a stronger sense of self-worth. Affirmations serve not only as reminders of our inherent value but also as catalysts for behavior changes that align with our goals and aspirations.

Incorporating affirmations into daily routines can enhance mindfulness and self-acceptance. When we engage in this practice, we train our minds to focus on the positive aspects of ourselves and our lives, rather than dwelling on perceived shortcomings. For individuals who struggle with negative self-perceptions, affirmations can provide a powerful counter-narrative, fostering a sense of empowerment. By regularly affirming our strengths, we create a mental environment conducive to personal growth and resilience, enabling us to approach challenges with confidence and clarity.

The effectiveness of affirmations is further amplified when they are combined with self-reflection techniques such as journaling. Writing down affirmations allows for deeper engagement with the messages we wish to internalize. This practice not only reinforces our commitment to personal development but also serves as a tangible record of our journey towards self-discovery. Journaling can reveal patterns in our thoughts and feelings, helping to identify areas where affirmations may need adjustment or where additional support may be required. This iterative process encourages continuous growth and self-improvement.

Building healthy relationships, both with ourselves and others, is another critical aspect of harnessing the power of affirmations. When individuals express positive affirmations about their worth, they cultivate a healthier self-image that influences how they interact with others. This self-assuredness fosters authentic connections and enhances communication, allowing for more meaningful relationships. Additionally, affirmations can serve as a tool for resolving conflicts or addressing insecurities within relationships, as they encourage individuals to articulate their needs and boundaries with confidence.

Ultimately, the journey of self-discovery is enriched by the consistent practice of affirmations. As we acknowledge our worth and embrace our unique qualities, we empower ourselves to navigate life's challenges with grace and resilience. The integration of affirmations into our daily lives not only bolsters our self-confidence but also inspires a broader perspective on our capabilities and potential. By embracing this transformative practice, we lay the foundation for a fulfilling and empowered existence, paving the way for a life characterized by authenticity, connection, and ongoing personal growth.

Creating Personalized Affirmations

Creating personalized affirmations is a powerful practice that can significantly enhance self-worth and foster a deeper understanding of one's value. To embark on this journey, it is essential to first reflect on your core beliefs and values. Take time to identify the areas in your life where you seek growth or healing, whether it be in relationships, career confidence, or overcoming feelings of inadequacy. This process involves introspection and honest self-assessment, allowing you to pinpoint the specific thoughts and feelings that may be holding you back. By acknowledging these challenges, you set the foundation for crafting affirmations that resonate with your unique experiences and aspirations.

Once you have a clear understanding of the beliefs you wish to transform, begin drafting affirmations that reflect your desired mindset. These statements should be positive, present tense, and personal, serving as a declaration of your worth and capabilities. For instance, instead of saying, "I will be confident," rephrase it to "I am confident and capable in my abilities." This shift in language reinforces the belief that you already possess the qualities you aspire to embody. Ensure that your affirmations are specific and actionable, as this clarity will empower you to integrate them into your daily routine effectively.

Incorporating these affirmations into your life requires consistency and dedication. Consider starting your day by reciting your personalized affirmations, either aloud or in written form. This practice not only sets a positive tone for the day but also reinforces your commitment to self-discovery and personal growth. Journaling can be an effective tool for this purpose; maintaining a dedicated space in your journal for your affirmations allows for reflection and tracking your progress. As you regularly engage with these statements, they begin to reshape your thoughts and influence your behaviors, fostering greater self-acceptance and resilience against imposter syndrome.

Awakening Your Inner Worth: A Journey to Self-Discovery

Moreover, it is beneficial to create an environment that supports your affirmations. Surround yourself with visual reminders, such as post-it notes or vision boards, that display your affirmations prominently. This constant exposure can help solidify your new mindset and serve as a reminder of your inner worth, especially during challenging moments. Engaging in mindfulness practices, such as meditation or deep breathing, can also enhance your connection to these affirmations, allowing you to internalize their meanings and feel their impact on your emotional well-being.

Finally, remember that the journey of self-discovery is ongoing, and your affirmations may evolve as you grow and learn more about yourself. Regularly reassess your statements to ensure they align with your current goals and values. This adaptive approach not only keeps your affirmations relevant but also encourages a deeper exploration of your identity and worth. Embrace the transformative power of personalized affirmations as a tool for empowerment and creative expression, guiding you through life's transitions and enriching your relationships with yourself and others.

Integrating Positive Self-Talk into Daily Life

Integrating positive self-talk into daily life is a transformative practice that can significantly enhance one's sense of self-worth and value. It begins with the simple recognition of the internal dialogue that shapes our thoughts and behaviors. Often, this inner voice may lean towards criticism and negativity, reinforcing feelings of inadequacy or self-doubt. By consciously shifting this dialogue to a more positive and affirming tone, individuals can cultivate a mindset that not only acknowledges their inherent worth but also empowers them to embrace their unique qualities and strengths.

To effectively integrate positive self-talk, it is essential to first identify the negative patterns that may have become ingrained over time. Keeping a journal can be an invaluable tool in this process. By documenting thoughts and feelings, individuals can gain insight into recurring negative statements that undermine their confidence. Reflecting on these entries allows one to challenge and reframe these thoughts into constructive affirmations. For instance, transforming "I am not good enough" into "I have unique strengths that contribute positively to my life and the lives of others" can create a powerful shift in perspective.

Awakening Your Inner Worth: A Journey to Self-Discovery

Incorporating positive self-talk into daily routines can further reinforce this new mindset. This can be accomplished through the use of affirmations, which serve as daily reminders of one's worth and capabilities. Setting aside time each day, perhaps during morning rituals or moments of quiet reflection, to recite these affirmations can significantly impact how individuals perceive themselves throughout the day. The repetition of positive statements not only helps to replace negative beliefs but also fosters a greater sense of self-acceptance and mindfulness, allowing individuals to navigate challenges with resilience and confidence.

Additionally, surrounding oneself with supportive and uplifting influences can amplify the effects of positive self-talk. Engaging in conversations with friends, mentors, or coaches who reinforce a positive narrative can help individuals internalize these affirmations more deeply. Furthermore, participating in personal development workshops or group activities that focus on building self-esteem and overcoming imposter syndrome can provide a sense of community and shared experience. These interactions not only validate one's journey but also encourage the practice of self-empowerment through creative expression and collaboration.

Ultimately, integrating positive self-talk into daily life is a continuous journey of self-discovery. It requires patience and commitment, but the rewards are profound. As individuals learn to embrace and articulate their worth, they not only enhance their personal development but also improve their relationships with others. By fostering a nurturing inner dialogue, individuals can navigate life transitions with greater ease and confidence, empowering themselves to thrive in all aspects of their lives. Through this practice, one can awaken a deeper sense of inner worth, setting the foundation for a fulfilling and authentic life.

Chapter 10: Navigating Life Transitions

Understanding Transition Phases

Awakening Your Inner Worth: A Journey to Self-Discovery

Understanding transition phases is a crucial aspect of personal development and self-discovery. Transitions are periods of change that can occur in various areas of life, including career shifts, relationship changes, or significant life events. Each transition phase presents unique challenges and opportunities for growth. Recognizing and understanding these phases can empower individuals to navigate them with greater resilience and clarity, ultimately leading to a deeper understanding of their self-worth.

The first phase of any transition often involves an ending, which can be characterized by feelings of loss and uncertainty. This phase may evoke emotions such as fear, anxiety, or sadness as individuals grapple with letting go of what is familiar. Acknowledging these feelings is essential; they are valid responses to change. Engaging in mindfulness practices can help individuals become more aware of their emotional landscape during this time, allowing for a more reflective approach to the transition. Journaling can also be beneficial, providing a safe space to explore and articulate thoughts and feelings about the ending phase, fostering a sense of acceptance.

Awakening Your Inner Worth: A Journey to Self-Discovery

Following the ending phase is often a period of exploration and uncertainty. During this time, individuals may find themselves questioning their identity and values as they seek to redefine their paths. This phase can be ripe for self-discovery, as individuals are encouraged to explore new possibilities and challenge limiting beliefs, such as those associated with imposter syndrome. Embracing creative expression can facilitate this exploration, allowing individuals to experiment with different aspects of themselves and their aspirations. It is essential to maintain a growth mindset during this phase, viewing challenges as opportunities for personal development rather than insurmountable obstacles.

As individuals progress through the transition, they may enter a phase of reorientation, where they begin to establish new routines and relationships that align with their evolving sense of self. This phase is crucial for building healthy relationships, as individuals learn to communicate their needs and boundaries more effectively. Engaging in personal development workshops or coaching can provide valuable insights and tools for navigating this phase. Additionally, positive self-talk and affirmations can reinforce self-worth, helping individuals embrace their new identities with confidence and clarity.

Finally, the transition culminates in a phase of integration, where individuals synthesize their experiences and insights into a cohesive sense of self. This phase is marked by acceptance of both the journey and the growth that has occurred. Individuals may feel a renewed sense of empowerment as they recognize their inherent worth and value. The lessons learned through the transition can lead to profound changes in how they approach future challenges and opportunities. By embracing the full spectrum of transition phases, individuals can cultivate a deeper understanding of themselves, ultimately enhancing their self-worth and fostering resilience in the face of change.

Coping Strategies for Change

Coping with change is an inevitable part of life, and understanding how to navigate these transitions is crucial for personal growth and self-worth. Individuals often face changes that can evoke feelings of uncertainty, anxiety, or even fear. By developing effective coping strategies, one can not only manage these feelings but also emerge stronger and more self-aware. Embracing change as an opportunity for self-discovery allows individuals to recognize their resilience and adaptability, reinforcing their inherent worth.

One of the most effective coping strategies for navigating change is mindfulness. Practicing mindfulness helps individuals stay present in the moment, allowing them to observe their thoughts and feelings without judgment. This practice can be particularly beneficial during times of transition, as it encourages a deeper understanding of one's emotions and reactions. By focusing on the here and now, individuals can reduce anxiety and foster a sense of calm, which is essential when facing the unknown.

Journaling serves as another powerful tool for coping with change. Writing about experiences, thoughts, and feelings can facilitate self-reflection and provide clarity during tumultuous times. Journaling encourages individuals to articulate their emotions, which can lead to greater self-awareness and understanding. Additionally, it allows for the tracking of personal growth over time, reinforcing one's journey and highlighting progress made amidst challenges. This practice not only aids in processing emotions but also cultivates a sense of empowerment as individuals recognize their ability to navigate life's complexities.

Building healthy relationships is also a critical component of coping with change. Surrounding oneself with supportive individuals can provide solace and guidance during transitions. Engaging in open communication with friends, family, or mentors can foster a sense of belonging and validation, which is essential for self-worth. Furthermore, these relationships can serve as a sounding board for thoughts and feelings, allowing for shared experiences and mutual encouragement. By leaning on a supportive network, individuals can feel less isolated and more confident in their ability to handle change.

Finally, affirmations and positive self-talk play a significant role in managing the emotional turmoil that often accompanies change. By consciously replacing negative self-perceptions with affirming statements, individuals can cultivate a more positive mindset. This shift in thinking not only mitigates feelings of self-doubt but also reinforces the belief in one's intrinsic value. Empowering oneself through creative expression, whether through art, music, or writing, can further enhance this positive self-dialogue, making it easier to embrace change as a catalyst for personal development and self-discovery.

Embracing New Beginnings

Embracing new beginnings is a pivotal aspect of the journey toward self-discovery and personal growth. Life is replete with transitions that often challenge our sense of self-worth and value. As adults navigating complex emotional landscapes, we must recognize that each new beginning presents an opportunity to reassess our goals, redefine our identities, and cultivate a deeper understanding of who we are. By actively engaging in this process, we not only enhance our self-acceptance but also lay the groundwork for building healthier relationships with ourselves and others.

Awakening Your Inner Worth: A Journey to Self-Discovery

The first step in embracing new beginnings involves acknowledging the emotions that accompany change. Whether it is a career transition, the end of a relationship, or a shift in personal circumstances, these moments can evoke feelings of uncertainty and self-doubt. It is essential to confront these emotions head-on, allowing ourselves to feel and process them rather than suppressing or avoiding them. Mindfulness practices can be particularly beneficial during these times, enabling us to stay present and grounded as we navigate our feelings. Journaling can also serve as a powerful tool for self-reflection, helping to clarify our thoughts and emotions as we embark on new paths.

As we begin to embrace change, it is crucial to challenge the limiting beliefs that may arise, particularly the pervasive imposter syndrome that many adults experience. This phenomenon often leads us to feel undeserving of success and happiness, causing us to second-guess our abilities and achievements. By reframing our internal narratives through positive self-talk and affirmations, we can cultivate a mindset that embraces our worthiness. Engaging in personal development workshops and coaching can further equip us with the tools necessary to build confidence and overcome these detrimental thought patterns.

Building healthy relationships is another vital aspect of embracing new beginnings. As we evolve, the dynamics within our personal and professional lives may shift. It is important to evaluate the relationships that no longer serve us while fostering connections that align with our values and aspirations. Open communication and vulnerability are essential in nurturing these relationships, allowing us to express our needs and boundaries clearly. By surrounding ourselves with supportive individuals who uplift and empower us, we create an environment conducive to growth and exploration.

Finally, embracing new beginnings is an invitation to explore creative expression as a means of empowerment. Engaging in artistic endeavors, whether through writing, painting, or other forms of creativity, allows us to articulate our experiences and emotions in a tangible way. This process not only fosters self-discovery but also serves as a therapeutic outlet, helping us to navigate the complexities of life transitions. By embracing our creative selves, we affirm our worth and reinforce the notion that our journey is uniquely our own. Ultimately, embracing new beginnings is not merely about change; it is about embracing the fullness of our identities and stepping into a future defined by self-acceptance and resilience.

Chapter 11: Empowerment through Creative Expression

Exploring Different Forms of Creativity

Awakening Your Inner Worth: A Journey to Self-Discovery

Exploring different forms of creativity can serve as a powerful tool in the journey of self-discovery and personal development. Creativity is not confined solely to traditional artistic endeavors; it encompasses various expressions, including problem-solving, innovative thinking, and emotional expression. By recognizing and embracing these diverse modes of creativity, individuals can unlock new pathways for understanding themselves and enhance their overall sense of worth. This exploration invites adults to reflect on their unique creative inclinations and how they can be utilized to foster self-acceptance and empowerment.

One significant aspect of creativity lies in its ability to facilitate self-reflection. Engaging in creative activities, such as journaling or visual arts, allows individuals to express their thoughts and emotions in ways that words alone may not capture. This process can lead to profound insights about one's values, beliefs, and aspirations. For those grappling with imposter syndrome, creative expression offers a safe space to confront fears and insecurities, enabling individuals to articulate their experiences and recognize their inherent worth. By channeling their feelings into creative outlets, individuals can dismantle negative self-perceptions and cultivate a more compassionate view of themselves.

Creative problem-solving is another vital form of creativity that can enhance personal development. This approach encourages individuals to think outside the box and approach challenges from new angles. Whether in career transitions or personal relationships, the ability to innovate solutions can significantly boost confidence and resilience. Workshops that focus on developing creative thinking skills can empower participants to tackle obstacles with a renewed perspective, ultimately leading to healthier interactions and improved self-esteem. By honing these skills, adults can navigate life's complexities with greater ease and assurance.

Awakening Your Inner Worth: A Journey to Self-Discovery

Mindfulness practices can also intertwine with creativity, providing a fertile ground for self-discovery. Activities such as mindful drawing, creative writing, or even cooking can ground individuals in the present moment while allowing their imaginative faculties to flourish. These practices promote self-acceptance by encouraging individuals to embrace imperfections and appreciate the process of creation rather than fixating on the end result. In this context, creativity becomes a form of meditation, facilitating a deeper connection to oneself and fostering a sense of inner peace and worth.

In conclusion, exploring different forms of creativity is essential for adults seeking to enhance their self-worth and personal growth. By engaging in creative expression, individuals can confront their fears, develop innovative solutions, and practice mindfulness, all of which contribute to a richer understanding of themselves. This journey not only empowers individuals to embrace their unique talents but also strengthens their ability to build healthy relationships and navigate life's transitions with confidence. As creativity unfolds, it reveals the inherent value within each person, inviting them to step fully into their authentic selves.

The Therapeutic Benefits of Art

The therapeutic benefits of art extend far beyond mere aesthetics; they serve as a profound conduit for self-discovery and personal growth. Engaging in artistic endeavors allows individuals to explore their thoughts, feelings, and experiences in a unique way, facilitating a deeper understanding of themselves. This creative process acts as a mirror reflecting inner emotions, often unearthing hidden aspects of self-worth and value that may have been overlooked. Through painting, drawing, or even writing, individuals can confront and articulate their feelings, ultimately leading to enhanced self-awareness and acceptance.

Art also provides a vital space for emotional expression, particularly for those grappling with imposter syndrome or self-doubt. Many adults find it challenging to voice their insecurities and vulnerabilities. However, the act of creating art can serve as a safe outlet for these emotions. By transforming their feelings into visual or written forms, individuals can externalize their internal struggles, making it easier to process and understand them. This creative release not only diminishes the weight of those feelings but also cultivates a sense of empowerment as individuals reclaim their narrative through their artistic expressions.

Furthermore, art encourages mindfulness and presence, essential components of self-acceptance and personal development. When immersed in the creative process, individuals often enter a state of flow, where their focus shifts entirely to the act of creation. This immersion fosters a heightened awareness of the present moment, which can be incredibly grounding and therapeutic. By engaging in art mindfully, adults can cultivate a deeper connection to themselves, allowing for moments of introspection and reflection that are critical for personal growth and navigating life transitions.

Participating in art can also enhance social connections, contributing to healthier relationships. Group art activities, whether in workshops or community classes, create opportunities for collaboration and shared experiences. These interactions enable individuals to bond over mutual interests, fostering a sense of belonging and support. As participants share their artistic journeys and insights, they develop communication skills and empathy, essential for building strong, healthy relationships. This communal aspect of art reinforces the understanding that personal worth is not only an individual pursuit but also a shared experience.

Finally, the therapeutic benefits of art are complemented by the positive affirmations and self-talk that often accompany creative expression. As individuals engage in their art, they are frequently reminded of their capabilities and potential. The process of creating something meaningful serves as a powerful affirmation of self-worth, encouraging individuals to challenge negative self-perceptions and replace them with constructive thoughts. This transformative journey through art not only enhances personal development but also instills a lasting sense of confidence and resilience, empowering individuals to embrace their unique worth in all facets of life.

Sharing Your Creative Journey

Awakening Your Inner Worth: A Journey to Self-Discovery

Sharing your creative journey can serve as a powerful tool for self-discovery and empowerment. It allows you to articulate your experiences, reflect on your growth, and connect with others who may resonate with your narrative. By documenting your path, whether through writing, art, or any form of expression, you create a tangible representation of your inner landscape, which can foster a deeper understanding of your self-worth and value. This process not only reinforces your identity but also encourages you to embrace your unique experiences, ultimately leading to greater self-acceptance.

Engaging in the act of sharing opens the door to vulnerability, which is often a catalyst for meaningful relationships. When you share your journey, you invite others into your world, allowing for authentic connections based on mutual understanding and empathy. This exchange can be transformative, as it shifts the focus from self-doubt and imposter syndrome to collective support and encouragement. By fostering an environment where stories are shared, we build communities that celebrate each individual's path and acknowledge the common struggles we face in our quests for self-acceptance and confidence.

Incorporating mindfulness into your creative sharing process enhances the impact of your narrative. Mindfulness encourages you to be present in the moment, allowing you to fully engage with your thoughts and feelings as you create. This heightened awareness not only aids in personal development but also enriches the stories you choose to share. By reflecting on your experiences with a mindful approach, you can better articulate your insights and the lessons learned throughout your journey, making your narrative more relatable and profound for others.

Journaling serves as an excellent method for articulating your creative journey. It provides a private space to explore your thoughts, document your emotions, and reflect on your progress. Regularly writing about your experiences can reveal patterns and insights that contribute to your self-discovery. Furthermore, sharing excerpts from your journal with trusted friends or in workshops can initiate discussions that deepen your understanding of your worth and value. This practice not only enhances your self-awareness but also encourages a culture of openness and growth among peers.

Lastly, embracing your creative expression as part of your self-discovery journey empowers you to navigate life transitions with confidence. Whether you are facing changes in your career, relationships, or personal goals, your creative work can serve as a guiding light. By sharing your experiences through various mediums, you not only affirm your own journey but also inspire others to embark on their paths of self-exploration. Empowerment through creative expression fosters resilience, allowing you to tackle challenges with a renewed sense of purpose and affirmation, ultimately reinforcing the belief in your inherent worth.